SUPPORT BEYOND THE CYCLE

SUPPORT BEYOND THE CYCLE

BRANDYN MCELROY

J Merrill Publishing, Inc., Columbus 43207
www.JMerrill.pub

Copyright © 2021 J Merrill Publishing, Inc.
All rights reserved. No part of this publication may be reproduced, distributed, or transmitted in any form or by any means, including photocopying, recording, or other electronic or mechanical methods, without the prior written permission of the publisher, except in the case of brief quotations embodied in critical reviews and certain other noncommercial uses permitted by copyright law. For permission requests, contact J Merrill Publishing, Inc., 434 Hillpine Drive, Columbus, OH 43207
Published 2021

Library of Congress Control Number: 2021904452
ISBN-13: 978-1-950719-96-9 (Paperback)
ISBN-13: 978-1-950719-95-2 (eBook)

Title: Support Beyond the Cycle
Author: Brandyn McElroy
Cover Artwork: Steven Withers

For my Family

CONTENTS

Introduction ix
Our Story xi

1. Your desire to have a child 1
2. The Road is long 3
3. Gather together 5
4. Supporting your wife 7
5. You are NOT your strength 9
6. Love through the pain 11
7. Battles will happen 13
8. Put down your steel and pick up your sword 15
9. Keeping God First 17
10. Reminder to Pray 19
11. Your allies 21
12. Take time to cry 23
13. He will never put more on you than you can bear 25
14. Your leadership she will follow 27
15. The miracle 29
16. His way 31
17. Reminder to study 33
18. Embody the fruit - Part 1 35
19. Embody the fruit - Part 2 37
20. Embody the fruit - Part 3 39
21. Go at this together 41
22. Your words matter 43
23. Protect her 45
24. Seek his will 47
25. Trust that it is his will 49
26. Reminder to Pray, again 51
27. Fear will show itself, be ready 53
28. Reminder to study, again 55
29. Be the man of God for your household 57

30. Closure of this chapter in life	59
Epilogue	61

The partner book to **Faith Beyond the Cycle**, written by my beautiful wife, Chanelle McElroy, for the Lady in your life that you are on this journey with.

This is for the husbands and soon to be fathers that are suffering from infertility. We are often forgotten about, not on purpose or out of neglect but simply out of the need to be strong for our wives and mothers to be. We often forget about our own needs to restore and rejuvenate, becoming exhausted and potentially ready to give up.

Although you may be feeling as if God has forgotten you, my brother, he truly has not. He is preparing you for what is to come. Your child will not be like other children, not in the mere sense that they are individuals but the fact that the testimony that leads to their conception and birth is much different from their counterparts.

> There hath no temptation taken you but such as is common to man: but God is faithful, who will not suffer you to be tempted above that ye are able; but will with the temptation also make a way to escape, that ye may be able to bear it.
>
> 1 CORINTHIANS 10:13

Your family's story is one that is unique but not alone. God has provided all the strength we need to make it through the temptation of quitting, suicide, divorce, and adultery.

Come with me on this journey to rejuvenation and strength.

May the Lord continue to bless you.

- Brandyn L. McElroy

OUR STORY

Fellas, let me be honest that in this book, there is a lot of emotion. For that, be thankful and grateful.

This book is to help you LET IT OUT. I know that we are the ones that must keep it together. We must be willing and able to bottle up our own emotion and accept our wives on top of. There are moments that we cry together, but we can only do it (in our minds) for a few minutes so that we can pick her up off of the ground and put the pieces back together.

I had this same feeling three times in a row with my wife. We were married in 2016. Over the next 2.5 years, we suffered three miscarriages, two surgeries, and countless false starts trying to have a child. The emotional toll on my wife was devastating to the point that she nearly attempted suicide.

While being newlyweds and attempting to have a little one, we moved across the country, expanded our roles and responsibilities at our 9-5 jobs, and started a new business together. To say the least, we had a lot going on.

OUR STORY

My wife was diagnosed with endometriosis and PCOS. Either diagnosis will make having a little one extremely difficult, let alone having a diagnosis with both. I felt there was never a right time to settle with my own emotions and feelings of loss, coupled with the loss of my grandfather and a dear uncle, all within a very short amount of time.

Struggling to make it was an understatement. Not having friends who truly understood the feeling and the impact of losing a child not once or twice but three times only made the situation much worse. The feeling that there was NO place to go and NO one to turn to.

There became times I felt that the only way to end this pain was to divorce and start over. Try to find another path around to the family I had dreamed of. I began to question myself, even saying I missed a sign somewhere; maybe my wife was not the woman for me?

I found myself warring with the devil, it seemed at every waking minute. I talked to friends trying to figure out what I needed to do to truly get myself together.

I began to really reach out to God... Not reach; cry, scream, sob out to God begging for help and strength. I began reading my Word more and truly asking God to come into my studies to show me what I needed to do for myself and my family.

There were still countless nights of battling the devil, yet now with some armor and guidance from God's Word. I felt stronger to make it through our situation.

There were nights I still felt alone or isolated in what I was dealing with. But I knew from growing up in a praying family that I was never truly alone, even when no one was around.

Prayer is one of the most powerful tools I found in my belt during this fight. Praying fervently and having the faith to know if I remained focused on God, I would get there.

OUR STORY

Through each miscarriage, my armor was tested and tried. I prayed harder for help in assisting my wife, and the Lord led me night after night to scriptures to help us get through.

My flesh struggled some nights with the emotions and not being able to let out the pain and fear in a way that made sense. I tried to fill the pain with material things such as a house and cars; focus on finance and career growth. But it still wasn't enough to satisfy my flesh and desire to become a father.

I found myself driving down a desert highway in New Mexico screaming out to God, WHY CAN'T I BE A FATHER?! Yet the small voice of God saying softly, "In time, my son," was always present.

September of 2018, I found myself in Phoenix, AZ, on a business trip, struggling to deal with all of the pressure when I thought I finally might give up on it all. My wife and I had been arguing nonstop from the time I left the house to head to the airport through the first 2 days of my trip. It had gotten to the point that I felt my spirit could no longer hold back my mind that this marriage was not going to work.

I began planning to return to my home in New Mexico and divorce my wife because there was war, it seemed, in the camp. She was angry, I was angry, but God was still present and spoke to me through prayer and meditation. I studied and prayed for the remainder of my trip, asking God to guide me, keep me, don't let me just "react."

He reminded me that I am his son and that I have been going about this the wrong way. I have been looking at it solely from what I want and not what HE wants for me. I was trying my hardest to do it all on my own rather than fully commit it all to him. Fully give him control over my desire and my family.

On my flight home, he showed me where the pains of not letting go of my emotions, with the passing of my children, grandfather, and uncle

OUR STORY

was killing me with stress and grief. This left me unavailable to my wife in the ways that she needed.

When I got home, my wife and I sat down and prayed. We reaffirmed our love for one another and recommitted ourselves to the mission of spreading God's Word and helping others see what God can and will do. My wife felt the leading of the spirit to start her book "Faith Beyond the Cycle" and that if she was obedient, her womb would be blessed.

October of 2018, my wife's womb was touched. Miraculously, this was just a month before we took further action with infertility treatments that our doctors had recommended. We were excited but nervous due to our history of losing children.

Yet, one day in November, we saw our "peanut" was beginning to grow and take form. This alone was a miracle enough for us to know that God was real and would take us through what we believed would be a smooth pregnancy and that we would soon welcome a baby girl in the summer of 2019. However, again our faith was about to be tested. It became necessary for me to step up and bear the emotional response to our little one's birth. But that's another story for truly another day.

Take this next 30 days to get a hold of your connection with God and understand your position, not just as a husband but the main conduit of blessings in your home through your faith in God.

DAY 1

YOUR DESIRE TO HAVE A CHILD

Asking for the Lord to bless us is common knowledge in our society today. Yet we must know that there are expectations from us as men to truly obtain the end blessing. We must first make sure that our connection with God is secure. Ensure our lives are aligned with his purpose and vision for us.

Once we solidify the connection, we must make sure that we have the faith to endure. You cannot find yourself wavering back and forth in your ability to trust God. When you ask for this blessing, make sure you're ready for the work that goes along with it.

To have a child is one of the most basic but rewarding blessings that a family desires. When that blessing seems to be delayed and not coming to fruition, it becomes easy to fall off the wagon of faith and trust in God.

Our wives are looking at us to be the hero, the strong wall, and we hope to be just that. As a man, we like to instinctually find solutions to the issues that come to each cycle. Yet over and over again, there is no sign of a child. It can become taxing, and a child can seem even further in the distance.

However, we must not forget to have FAITH. Don't give up on God's plan as he is not giving up on you as long as you remain fully connected in him and don't waiver.

> *But let him ask in faith, nothing wavering. For he that wavereth is like a wave of the sea driven with the wind and tossed. For let not that man think that he shall receive any thing of the Lord. A double minded man is unstable in all his ways.*
>
> JAMES 1:6-8

DAY 2

THE ROAD IS LONG

Day after day, night after night, the desire for this little one to come drags on. Your desire has been the same, your prayer has been the same, and your faith has not wavered. Your connection with God and your family is strong, yet you're still not there.

The blessed news of a little one coming into your lives has not happened, or even harder still, you've lost a little one in the process of development. Remember, my brother, that the road is a long one.

However, at the end of this road will be a testimony like none other.

Where is the benefit in that? The benefit is growth and development for your little one, patience, and stronger faith for you and your spouse to triumph in the many difficult situations ahead.

We often look at the destination and don't even expect, let alone pay attention to the journey. Have you taken a step back and considered that the Lord may be preparing you for what is to come?

After birth may be the long road of NICU or Physical therapy, challenges unseen, and at times unheard of. However, this time of patience is teaching you to take every moment and appreciate it.

In the end, his plan will prevail, and your blessing will be revealed and delivered to you. Remember to communicate with your wife, "the road is long, but together with God, we WILL make it through.

We must maintain our patience." Be open and honest about your feelings with her, and she will feel more confident in your patience and strength.

> *Knowing this, that the trying of your faith worketh patience. But let patience have her perfect work, that ye may be perfect and entire, wanting nothing.*
>
> JAMES 1:3-4

DAY 3

GATHER TOGETHER

You are the protector of your wife and your home. You are doing all that you can to protect her and comfort her. In many cases, this can be hiding away, staying alone and quiet, removed, and almost exiled from the outside world. However, my brother, I will share, it is important to find an outlet.

Family members, friends, and support groups are good but ensure that they can connect on a spiritual level. There is strength and guidance in groups. There are things you will not share with your wife out of fear of seeming weak or unsupportive and vice versa.

Having a couple in your corner that has been there or are a strong rock in the Lord is more important than ever. Initially, your thoughts will be a place to vent and share frustrations. But what can and will evolve is a deeper relationship with each other, the couple, and, more importantly, God.

As brothers and sisters in Christ, coming together can be uplifting, even if it's just for prayer and a hug to acknowledge the unspoken pain.

BRANDYN MCELROY

My brother, don't feel like you have to do this alone. Pray and ask God to show you the RIGHT couple to join up with to be your faith partners, walking and talking with you in this journey.

Be open and willing to share so that you're able to feel the relief and release you need.

> *Not forsaking the assembling of ourselves together, as the manner of some is; but exhorting one another: and so much the more, as ye see the day approaching.*
>
> HEBREWS 10: 25

DAY 4

SUPPORTING YOUR WIFE

To support your wife, you must first make sure that you are supported. A bridge must be anchored to uphold the loads it carries day in and day out. So, the question is, are you firmly anchored? If you're anchored in God, that is the best foundation any individual and family can have.

Next, your support cables must be in place to help with the transferring of weight as the days go on. Ensure that your outlets are there and find constructive ways to let out the stress, pain, and fear. Do you have an empty bridge (mind) deck, clear and ready to go for transporting the ins and outs of emotions from your spouse?

As men, we tend to think of being physically present as enough to say we're supportive. Sadly, if your mind's bridge deck is cluttered with other concerns, worries, and distractions, we cannot have a healthy flow of support for our wives. Clear your mind and be ready.

Finally, make sure that lanes are clearly marked, allowing for communication to flow. Communication is important when you are struggling to make it through as a couple. Suppose you're not vulnerable with her or open to clearly communicate with her. In that case, it will be a one-way flow of thoughts and emotion, leading to an overload on either person.

Remember that God brought your two together. Not by happenstance but for a purpose. Although things are difficult at times, your lives are now codependent. You must be anchored, supported, clear-minded, and ready for communication to ensure you're supporting your wife. In turn, you'll find you can support much more than you could have ever imagined. Leading to a much happier and comfortable home.

> *Whoso findeth a wife findeth a good thing, and obtaineth favour of the LORD. Matthew 19:5-6 (KJV) And said, For this cause shall a man leave father and mother, and shall cleave to his wife: and they twain shall be one flesh? Wherefore they are no more twain, but one flesh. What therefore God hath joined together, let not man put asunder.*
>
> PROVERBS 18:22 KJV

DAY 5

YOU ARE NOT YOUR STRENGTH

Shockingly enough, you are not your strength (ha). Although this may seem obvious, you will and have forgotten it already. It is important in the moments of fear, pain, and distress to remember this.

It becomes very easy for us men to find ourselves discouraged, depressed, and defeated.

God is the source of the power that drives the strength you possess. He has brought you through all of the trails thus far and will continue to bring you out as long as you follow him and reverence him as the source.

Understanding God's great power and love for you may seem hard at times, but all of this is to make you stronger and firmer in knowing to go to him and not lean on yourself or others for strength. It's a simple equation God = Strength.

You're no less of a man for accepting it. Embrace it, and you will find it much easier to accept his power and the peace it brings for you and your spouse.

BRANDYN MCELROY

> *I will lift up mine eyes unto the hills, from whence cometh my help. My help cometh from the LORD, which made heaven and earth.*
>
> PSALMS 121:1-2 KJV

DAY 6

LOVE THROUGH THE PAIN

You get to know pain throughout this process. Remember that "It is ok to not be ok" in the moment. Pain from the loss of a child can be nearly unbearable; add to that your spouse's pain.

Remember that through all of these struggles and battles, the Lord is with you. It is important to again to draw from your strength God. Be kind and gentle to your spouse even though you are likewise finding it difficult to deal with.

As the head of the house, you must find the right words and or actions to provide love through this moment. Our spouses have an overwhelming amount of hormones, emotions, and physical pains that we will never understand.

If we take the typical male stance of tough love or fix the issue, we can make it worse. Even in the mocking, scorning, and a walk of shame to death, Christ loved us. He showed it in his restraint, his continued participation in the practice of crucifixion.

BRANDYN MCELROY

If Christ can love us (those he's never physically met) enough to die for us, can we not love our spouses enough to pray for and with them and show them, true love. God's Love.

> *And when they had platted a crown of thorns, they put it upon his head, and a reed in his right hand: and they bowed the knee before him, and mocked him, saying, Hail, King of the Jews!*
>
> MATTHEW 27:27-31 KJV

DAY 7

BATTLES WILL HAPPEN

Emotions are real. You have them, and we both know your wife does as well. However, there are times when the clash in emotions is inevitable.

What do you do when tempers flare, and it seems that you have a choice to make? Choose to not sin.

It is easy in these trying times to want to step out on your wife and be with someone else. Thoughts of finding something else can arise, and you may even be tempted to do it by the enemy. Just don't do it.

Your emotions are different from hers in some ways. You will often seek to find a solution fast and try to make her do the same. At this moment, your intentions are good, and you're truly trying to help, but it seems as if she does not care nor have a desire to understand your point of view.

That temptation of a Facebook message, Instagram direct message, text, or extra "hello" at work may seem like a good out. However, it will only bring further pain and destruction to you both. Understand that in this moment, it's ok for you not to be ok, as well it's ok for her to be that too.

When tempers flare, be the one that stops and evaluates and brings things back to calm. Your wife will be looking for that from you, although she may not say it verbally.

Your guidance and leadership matters, and your decisions to stay sin-free even when temptations strike makes the difference.

> *Be ye angry, and sin not: let not the sun go down upon your wrath: Neither give place to the devil.*
>
> EPHESIANS 4:26-27 KJV

DAY 8

PUT DOWN YOUR STEEL AND PICK UP YOUR SWORD

Your words matter. More than anything else in this process, your word matters to God, you, and your spouse. It can become easy to become frustrated, discouraged, and angry, as we have discussed; however, your mightiest weapon is your tongue.

Understanding that your words can bring life and death to the mood of your marriage and this process is key. The Bible often speaks of the power of the tongue, and it is no different in this situation.

Instead of lashing out in frustration, speak life into your spouse. Instead of saying why us Lord, be grateful for the test and the end results of God's promises. Instead of telling yourself you cannot deal with this situation, speak positivity about the journey you have endured thus far.

Your words will guide the thoughts and decisions to come. Be prepared to press forward with God's help and assistance.

Communicate your concerns and fears but do not dwell in them or use them to cause harm to yourself or your relationships with God and your spouse.

BRANDYN MCELROY

> *Death and life are in the power of the tongue: and they that love it shall eat the fruit thereof.*
>
> PROVERBS 18:21 KJV

DAY 9

KEEPING GOD FIRST

Tomorrow is God's to control.

We get so wrapped up in planning, tracking, and monitoring during these times. Looking for answers, wondering when, and trying to figure out the path forward.

Instead, we should be focused on one thing... God. He has already laid out the path for what is to come, yet we can't seem to be ok with trusting in him.

Is it because he doesn't answer us directly by picking up the phone and calling or sending a text? Is it because we want so badly to say we're in control of this situation when it is clear that we are not?

My brother, for all of the planning and forethought, you cannot and will not be prepared for every step along this journey. However, you can relieve yourself of the burdens of tomorrow. You can lift the weight of the future and what it holds by giving it all back to the one that determines it.

Stop looking to be God's mind reader and instead put your mind in his word. Draw strength from what he has already done and shown you.

Be ok with reading his word vs. looking for the next new doctor. Be ok with reading a daily scripture vs. tracking daily cycles. It will come when he is ready, and you must be ok with it.

The sooner you keep God first and let him lead... the sooner you realize he's got this whole thing already mapped out.

> *But seek ye first the kingdom of God, and his righteousness; and all these things shall be added unto you. Take therefore no thought for the morrow: for the morrow shall take thought for the things of itself. Sufficient unto the day is the evil thereof.*
>
> MATTHEW 6:33-34 KJV

DAY 10

REMINDER TO PRAY

Find a plan for prayer. Prayer is like the blood vessels that run through your body. It carries the hopes, dreams, desires, needs, anxiety, stress, and conversations directly to the ear of God.

We would not be able to live without the blood vessels traveling through our bodies, carrying our life resources back and forth. Neither does your salvation if we are not in constant communication with God in our prayer life.

Do not give up on it. Do not get distracted from it. Do it with your spouse and alone.

Pray when you first wake (before getting out of bed), pray on your drive to work, pray when you arrive, and pray throughout the day. Give prayers of thanks when leaving work and continue the prayers when your wife or family makes it home.

Finally, pray as the final thing you do before closing your eyes. As the prayers continue to flow, it is easier to walk and talk with God.

It becomes easier to leave your burdens with him because you'll know that he has and will continue to bless. Once you finish prayer throughout the day, make sure that you rejoice and show gratitude.

The Father knows that your faith and trust is in his ability to answer the "Prayer line."

> *Rejoice evermore. Pray without ceasing. In every thing give thanks: for this is the will of God in Christ Jesus concerning you.*
>
> 1 THESSALONIANS 5:16-18 KJV

DAY 11

YOUR ALLIES

Who are your prayer warriors?

Find yourself and your family a team of prayer warriors that can be agreed in prayer on your desires. The Lord has already told us that if we come together with a petition, he will hear it.

Stand on his promise and have the faith that your petition will be heard. Ensure that your prayer warriors agree with your prayer. Unified prayer is strength.

Notice in the word the Lord doesn't tell us to put out our furthest reaching tweet, Facebook message, or Instagram post. He says to us throughout that if there be a few gathered in his name, he'd be there.

Being there with you means you have salvation and the faith that he is with you at that moment.

BRANDYN MCELROY

> *Again I say unto you, That if two of you shall agree on earth as touching any thing that they shall ask, it shall be done for them of my Father which is in heaven. For where two or three are gathered together in my name, there am I in the midst of them.*
>
> MATTHEW 18:19-20 KJV

DAY 12

TAKE TIME TO CRY

As men, we try to hide the pains that we are suffering, reserving our tears for quiet and alone time. Whether in the shower, driving to work, or in the man cave for the game. Understand that it IS OK TO CRY.

Whatever macho fantasy you're living in, throw it out. You cannot be available to your spouse if you are filled with emotion and grief. Have this crying moment alone when needed but be open to having it together.

Grief is a healer, whether we realize it or not. It is a natural emotion that everyone has and recognizes in others. Let it out.

Remember that after the grief comes joy. After the pain comes the promise of a better and brighter tomorrow.

Give thanks to God for what is and praise him for what you have faith will be. Remind your spouse of the same and bring your bond closer together in these moments.

BRANDYN MCELROY

> *Sing unto the LORD, O ye saints of his, and give thanks at the remembrance of his holiness. For his anger endureth but a moment; in his favour is life: weeping may endure for a night, but joy cometh in the morning.*
>
> PSALMS 30:4-5 KJV

DAY 13

HE WILL NEVER PUT MORE ON YOU THAN YOU CAN BEAR

The enemy of our souls is never too far away, especially in times of trial.

When your path does not seem clear, the enemy will throw additional dirt on the road. At times it may seem to lead you on a path that is pleasing, violent, or in plain against that of your heavenly father.

My brother, understand this, No situation is worth losing your salvation over. Even when the trials seem as dark as midnight, know that you always have God on your side.

Remember that following the enemy even in tough times is a choice. He cannot force you to decide to follow his deceptions.

God has a way of always providing an exit to whatever trap the devil may provide. Your decision-making skills may seem numb because of the hunt to make the right choice to build your family. However, you've been making the decision to follow God this whole time, so don't let this season be any different.

BRANDYN MCELROY

There hath no temptation taken you but such as is common to man: but God is faithful, who will not suffer you to be tempted above that ye are able; but will with the temptation also make a way to escape, that ye may be able to bear it.

1 CORINTHIANS 10:13 KJV

DAY 14

YOUR LEADERSHIP SHE WILL FOLLOW

Your spouse will follow you, but only if you are being led by God.

In relationships, many just look at the woman as a being to be submissive to the husband without fail. However, I implore you, brother, to think differently.

No woman, especially a child of God, will follow blindly. Nor should you lead blindly.

It is important to remember the order of command in relationships that lead to a successful family. God is the head, Christ leads the man, and the man leads the woman and family. If you miss a link in that chain, it becomes broken and or torn.

It is hard for a woman to trust and believe if her husband is not following Christ. Ultimately it could cause a delay in the granting of your desires if you are not following Christ and the heavenly father in your life and in your decisions.

The longer you wait to restore the order, the longer this journey could be. The children of Israel learned this hard lesson, and many perished before seeing the promise of God come true.

Don't be that one, my brother. Get your life and hierarchy in order. Study together with your wife and lead by example when it comes to serving Christ.

Once your house is in order, you can truly step out and receive God's blessings.

> *But I would have you know, that the head of every man is Christ; and the head of the woman is the man; and the head of Christ is God.*
>
> 1 CORINTHIANS 11:3 KJV

DAY 15

THE MIRACLE

God is still in the miracle business. Sometimes it can be hard to understand the delay in a blessing and why you're the one that seems to be "suffering." But, remember that God does everything in His perfect will.

Your little one already has a blessing on their life. There is already a purpose for this soon to be miracle child, and we just have to trust that God is preparing us.

In our wait, it can seem as if we are getting to the point that the blessing with be missed because of earthly limitations or timelines.

God does not work on our earthly timelines. He does not bless based on when the doctors say it is "good" to have a child. He works on his agenda. This is why we must be aligned with him to better grasp his reasoning when it happens.

The miracle that you were born a child and now raising a family is a testimony to his powerful and mighty hand. You never know when your story may breathe life into someone else struggling to believe and have faith.

BRANDYN MCELROY

Don't give up or give in. Press forward with the understanding that your miracle is on schedule for God's clock.

> *And God said, Sarah thy wife shall bear thee a son indeed; and thou shalt call his name Isaac: and I will establish my covenant with him for an everlasting covenant, and with his seed after him.*
>
> GENESIS 17:19 KJV

DAY 16

HIS WAY

Our heavenly father has a way and a plan for our lives. Often we fight against it, especially when things seem to be going down a path we don't agree with.

Understand my brother that just because you don't see where he is taking you doesn't mean it isn't for your benefit.

Even though you know that at times you must remind yourself and your spouse often. This little one, this family, this plan will only come together in his time. You cannot rush it or try to make it happen sooner than God intends for it.

So, when you're feeling the pressure of your plan vs. Gods; or that things are out of control, Pray.

Pray that the Lord would help you to align to his plan. Ask that he would show you the way to go. Lay out your desires but understand that they are just that... desires. He may choose to delay their arrival.

God's got it, and you'll be just fine in the end.

BRANDYN MCELROY

> *After this manner therefore pray ye: Our Father which art in heaven, Hallowed be thy name. Thy kingdom come, Thy will be done in earth, as it is in heaven. Give us this day our daily bread. And forgive us our debts, as we forgive our debtors. And lead us not into temptation, but deliver us from evil: For thine is the kingdom, and the power, and the glory, forever. Amen.*
>
> MATTHEW 6:9-13

DAY 17

REMINDER TO STUDY

The Word of God is the sword and guide in your life. If it is not yet, then allow it to move to the front of the must-read list daily.

You may feel like I don't want to throw the Bible at everything; however, you are asking God daily for guidance, strength, peace, and so much more. He provides, at a minimum, his guidance in his text. Followed by your faith in him and your daily turning over of your life to him.

Read your guide so that you know how to navigate this life. Just like you don't go on a road trip without checking the distance and stops on google, don't try and fight the enemy, live happily, supply strength to your family, or any other thing without the guidance of your heavenly father.

Read your word, Brother, daily.

BRANDYN MCELROY

> *Study to shew thyself approved unto God, a workman that needeth not to be ashamed, rightly dividing the word of truth.*
>
> 2 TIMOTHY 2:15 KJV

DAY 18

EMBODY THE FRUIT - PART 1

This journey is a true test of you as an individual, your spirituality, and you as a husband. God does not allow anything to happen to us without the ability to provide an escape or a way to make it through.

Often, we hear in church the "fruits of the spirit" and think they sound good, but I can't achieve them. However, let me explain why you need them more than ever throughout this journey - working backward from how they are written in the Word.

- Temperance is to be able to restrain oneself or have self-control physically and emotionally. Having the ability to keep yourself in control in this situation is key. You cannot fly off the handle when needed to lead, stay strong for, or make decisions with and for your family. You must remain levelheaded and focused.
- Meekness is to be teachable, patient, and humble. You are ever learning during this trial about you, your wife, life as it is designed, and you will find that you do not understand all

that you thought you did. You must settle your ego and be teachable with your wife and the situation at hand.
- Faith is the substance of things hoped for, the evidence of things not seen (Heb 11:1). Your child has not arrived, your wife is breaking down, you are finding it more and more difficult to hold fast to God's promise. However, that is exactly the time that you need Faith. Trust in God, lay it all out to him, and watch what he does.

DAY 19

EMBODY THE FRUIT - PART 2

This journey is a true test of you as an individual, your spirituality, and you as a husband. God does not allow anything to happen to us without the ability to provide an escape or a way to make it through.

Often, we hear in church the "fruits of the spirit" and think they sound good, but I can't achieve them. However, let me explain why you need them more than ever throughout this journey.

- Goodness is the action of being "good." It becomes easy to act out of being negative in this long fight for what seems to be your right. You can become ill towards others' successful baby announcements, children, or even conversations. You must remain good. Showing the same goodness that your heavenly father shows to you daily by giving your life to fight another day. Not everyone is aware of your struggle and, therefore, may not treat you with the gentleness you need. However, it is still on you to be a kind and good person.

- Gentleness is helping others even when we have been wronged. Going along with being good is to be gentle; even with your own household, this situation's struggle hits everyone differently. Your wife may be more sensitive to the struggle and therefore need you to be calmer, simpler, and gentle with her. Not being able to take the direct and harsher realities of "tough love."
- Longsuffering is to patiently endure lasting hardship—some journeys to a new baby last month's others last years. However, we must not give up on God, just as he will not give up on you. We give God every reason at times to walk away from us and leave us to our own devices. However, he doesn't. He stays beside us. Loving us through the pain.

DAY 20

EMBODY THE FRUIT - PART 3

This journey is a true test of you as an individual, your spirituality, and you as a husband. God does not allow anything to happen to us without the ability to provide an escape or a way to make it through. Often, we hear in church the "fruits of the spirit" and think they sound good, but I can't achieve them. However, let me explain why you need them more than ever throughout this journey.

- Peace is more than just not fighting or it being quiet in the house. You must find and be the Peace in your home physically and spiritually, and in your life. The wonderful thing is finding it is simple. Turn to your father and give it all to him. Keeping it can be the test through trials, tribulations, and testing of your flesh during this process. Being the peace for your wife (in partnership with God) is your greatest challenge. Helping her in ways that will ease her stress and burden. Whether that's the laundry or helping to remind her to study her word at night. Be the peace you're seeking.

- Joy is the choice to see and exude happiness. Finding joy even in this challenge can change the entire outcome of your mental and spiritual state. It also leads to a positive impact on your wife as she works to make it through this, as well. You being joyful and happy signals to her that she can be at ease to some degree.
- Love is best described in 1 Cor 13:4-8 Charity suffereth long, and is kind; charity envieth not; charity vaunteth not itself, is not puffed up, Doth not behave itself unseemly, seeketh not her own, is not easily provoked, thinketh no evil; Rejoiceth not in iniquity, but rejoiceth in the truth; Beareth all things, believeth all things, hopeth all things, endureth all things. Charity never faileth: but whether there be prophecies, they shall fail; whether there be tongues, they shall cease; whether there be knowledge, it shall vanish away.

Embody these attributes, and you will find it hard to not have the tools your need to make it through this trial.

> *But the fruit of the Spirit is love, joy, peace, longsuffering, gentleness, goodness, faith, Meekness, temperance: against such there is no law.*
>
> GALATIANS 5:22-23

DAY 21

GO AT THIS TOGETHER

It is in the words of an R&B song, "Just the two of us." Remember that you and your wife are going through this together.

Yes, there are times and portions of this journey that seem more individual than joint but understand that it's both. Lean on one another and God only for help to make it through the trying times.

The worst thing you can do is invite outside (non-medical or spiritual) observation and conversation into the marriage. Although you will likely seek counsel from parents and close friends, remember that you have made a vow to do this together. Others may not be dealing with the same sensitivities or have the needed understanding to guide beyond comfort.

Trust in God and yourselves to make final decisions for your family moving forward. There will be times that others want to interject their opinions, but just like an argument about finances stays within the home, troubles and trials should be kept within the home.

BRANDYN MCELROY

Good intentions and gestures can become distractions or temptations to lean away even in the simplest areas. God, your wife, and you are more than capable of figuring this thing out.

Stay fervent in joint prayer and supplication to God. He will guide you better than anyone. Remember, he already knows the outcome.

> *And he answered and said unto them, have ye not read, that he which made them at the beginning made them male and female, And said, For this cause shall a man leave father and mother, and shall cleave to his wife: and they twain shall be one flesh? Wherefore they are no more twain, but one flesh. What therefore God hath joined together, let not man put asunder.*
>
> MATTHEW 19:4-6

DAY 22

YOUR WORDS MATTER

You are her EVERYTHING. Act like it.

Brother, we men tend to think that our words of "tough love" hit her ears and ring with the same truth and self-motivation as when others say them to us. However, that has never worked, and you know it.

Be gentle and kind; treat her as the queen you desire her to be. Step out of the hard outer shell and protector mode and into the warm and vulnerable. Your wife needs a tender touch and guidance.

If you always respond with tough and brittle, it will only push her to close in on herself and make her feel as if she is, even more, the problem. Struggling to produce a child for you both and struggling to show you the confidence you seem to demand.

When you were at your lowest point as a child and most sensitive, your mother (mother figure) would be the one that comes to you and helps nurture your emotions and feelings. This is the space your wife needs you to be in for her.

BRANDYN MCELROY

It may seem painful, trying, and tiring, but without this nurture, it will be a struggle for your wife to find the confidence needed to nurture the child in her womb you both desire.

> *So ought men to love their wives as their own bodies. He that loveth his wife loveth himself. For no man ever yet hated his own flesh; but nourisheth and cherisheth it, even as the Lord the church:*
>
> EPHESIANS 5:28-29 KJV

DAY 23

PROTECT HER

You will always protect her physical body and presence. It is in your nature's dedication to her as the husband to do so. However, many times where we miss protection as men is in the spiritual and mental realms.

This trial is spiritually draining, not in a negative in your trust and prayer overall. But in the sense that you have to always have your guard up, which can become burdensome.

For your wife, the constant borage of internal battles of, is it her fault or is it just not meant to be, can lead to a negative outlook and a lapse in trust in the heavenly Father. That is when you as the husband must step in to reassure through prayer, study, and encouragement. Your wife (as long as you remain led by God and connected) will naturally look to you for guidance. Be ready.

How is this protecting her? Your spiritual connection with God will be evident in your speech, your reading of his word, and even the night and morning prayers allowing her to gain spiritual energy to press on.

BRANDYN MCELROY

Mental health is real. Trying to process all of these emotions capped with the hormones from attempts to conceive can and will leave your wife in a tornado of uncertainty, eventually leading to break down without support.

Keeping her occupied with her hobbies and fun things is a simple way to help her maintain. Reminding her that things will work out to God's plan and that she cannot blame, plan, or figure out all that God has in store.

> *Husbands, love your wives, even as Christ also loved the church, and gave himself for it; That he might sanctify and cleanse it with the washing of water by the word,*
>
> EPHESIANS 5:25-26 KJV

DAY 24

SEEK HIS WILL

How often are we caught up in the thoughts of our own plans? Job, family, vehicles, houses, children, and so much more. However, we don't spend nearly as much time asking for his leadership, guidance, and just plainly his will.

We refuse at times to accept that God's will is truly the only thing that matters. We will push against this thought until God reveals it to us. When he reveals his plan, we often realize that we missed the whole journey, worried, concerned, or scared.

During this trial, my brother, I pray that you truly take every prayer to seek God's will first before making your request and when ending in your requests. Formality aside, you must believe that it is in his will.

Seeking God's will can allow the clearing of your mind to free you from rehashing your desires. Instead, you began to focus on what you already know is important - God's work and being a witness of him in all situations. Keeping God's will first in your life allows lower stress levels, which in turn can lead to mental and physical health benefits.

BRANDYN MCELROY

Seek God's will FIRST.

> *Pray without ceasing. In every thing give thanks: for this is the will of God in Christ Jesus concerning you.*
>
> 1 THESSALONIANS 5:17-18 KJV

DAY 25

TRUST THAT IT IS HIS WILL

God's will and your will can many times be headed in opposite or, at minimum, slightly different directions. Your ability to grasp what God has planned is, most of the time, rendered useless. However, it behooves us to TRUST in God's will and his way.

We far too often find ourselves spending hours worrying about how things will go to get you to your desired goal. Trust God's plan. If he already has a plan for your life, he has the means to ensure it will happen. You must trust him and follow his commandments.

When has God ever failed you? He may not have made it happen in your desired time frame; however, he has always been there when you've needed him.

This Trial is a part of the ultimate plan of your life. Be ok with the journey and trust God's will over you. Become settled in the comfort that God's got it, and you don't have to worry or complain.

This doesn't mean you won't have struggles but instead means your struggles have purpose and meaning.

BRANDYN MCELROY

Moreover whom he did predestinate, them he also called: and whom he called, them he also justified: and whom he justified, them he also glorified. What shall we then say to these things? If God be for us, who can be against us? He that spared not his own Son, but delivered him up for us all, how shall he not with him also freely give us all things?

ROMANS 8:30-32 KJV

DAY 26

REMINDER TO PRAY, AGAIN

Your knees hurt by now, that's ok. No Pain. No Gain.

Your time with God is so important. You spend hours researching the same products, procedures, cases, and issues about your situation. Still, you feel that you don't need to spend double, if not triple that, in prayer time?

God is our father and knows what we need and are looking for. Take the time to talk to him. He takes this time to hear our desires and shows our willingness to submit ourselves to him.

At some point, your heart and mind will feel that they no longer know what to ask for, how to pray, and maybe even for a moment forget what the true desire is. That's ok. The spirit within you knows, and it communicates with God.

Keep praying, and don't stop until change comes. Keep living for God and doing what he asks of you so that your prayers can go higher than the ceiling above you. It is essential to retain your salvation to be heard.

You can't just do what you want or fall to temptation without forgiveness to continue your prayer line. You can and will make it.

Now, pray.

> *Likewise the Spirit also helpeth our infirmities: for we know not what we should pray for as we ought: but the Spirit itself maketh intercession for us with groanings which cannot be uttered. And he that searcheth the hearts knoweth what is the mind of the Spirit, because he maketh intercession for the saints according to the will of God.*
>
> ROMANS 8:26-27 KJV

DAY 27

FEAR WILL SHOW ITSELF, BE READY

The enemy of your soul is lurking at every corner of this trial. Keep that in your mind there will be times where you will be pressed to the edge and will need to make the conscious decision to step back and evaluate.

Fear and failure will lead the charge throughout this chapter of your life. Remember that it calls for the entire armor of God to protect yourself.

In the wee hours of the morning, when it's just you and him, call out. Don't be afraid to seek God's help. In fact, it's a mandate to truly making this entire situation work.

Dealing with the enemy is not like dealing with low iron. You can't just pop a pill or eat some greens and replenish it. The enemy comes in different forms at different points in times, and the best way for him to get you is when you're backed against the wall.

The other opportune times the enemy comes in is when things seem to be going so well, and there's a setback. Don't give in to the temptation that says "it's over" or "see, I told you so."

BRANDYN MCELROY

Here again, fear and failure can set in and drive you to make decisions that go against your situation and your salvation. Hold firm to God's hand and put every level of protection you can between yourself, your family, and the enemy.

> *Put on the whole armour of God, that ye may be able to stand against the wiles of the devil. For we wrestle not against flesh and blood, but against principalities, against powers, against the rulers of the darkness of this world, against spiritual wickedness in high places.*
>
> EPHESIANS 6:11-12 KJV

DAY 28

REMINDER TO STUDY, AGAIN

Prayer is a critical line of communication between you and God. However, studying his word is the reminder or road map of abundant living in Christ Jesus.

Often we seek self-help books and top-rated authors to give us guidance in daily life.

That is good to help with continued learning and developing yourself. However, there is one book, and one road map to a successful go at abundant living through Christ, and that's the Bible. Studying is so key to our success. It's the time that you understand the trials and tribulations of those that have gone before you and God's guidance on what to do. What better way to make sure that you live life abundantly through God than to hear from him through his given word? Don't shortchange yourself. Laying out the blueprints for not only you but your entire family. Remember that you have to be the man, which is the connection between family as a whole and God.

All scripture is given by inspiration of God, and is

profitable for doctrine, for reproof, for correction, for instruction in righteousness: That the man of God may be perfect, thoroughly furnished unto all good works.

2 TIMOTHY 3:16-17

DAY 29

BE THE MAN OF GOD FOR YOUR HOUSEHOLD

God has called you brother to be his representation not only to your family but to those that may cross your path. Especially those that are/will be suffering through the trials that you and I have gone through to this point. Being a man of God goes beyond just your four walls as our lives today reach so many with different avenues.

My brother, you have the power to influence so many through the example that you set within your own home. Understanding God's will and desire for your life and walking in that purpose shines beyond the walls of your home and work.

Your wife will benefit from your constant obedience to God's will and way. She, too, will feel the spirit you possess and will desire to stand beside you in strength instead of allowing fear to grip and control her. Finally, your child (to be) will appreciate in later years your dedication to God.

Giving them the pathway to successfully living in faith, trusting in our everlasting father, and ensuring their road map is clear.

BRANDYN MCELROY

> *But I would have you know, that the head of every man is Christ; and the head of the woman is the man; and the head of Christ is God.*
>
> 1 CORINTHIANS 11:3

DAY 30

CLOSURE OF THIS CHAPTER IN LIFE

Through all of this, God is deserving of the glory.

Your life is a living testimony. It is a canvas to the goodness and will of God.

Let his praises ring from your voice, your walk on this earth, your marriage, and your fatherhood. God is the one that has made this happen, no matter the surgeries, the tears, the medical advice or actions, the treatments, and plans.

You've made it through the sleepless nights, the long drives with tears running down your face, the holding it together when you wanted to give up. You've triumphed over the darkness of the late nights with your wife in tears, the enemy whispering "give up," and the temptations put in your path.

You have allowed God to lead you, guide you, and protect you. It is now time to Pray. Study. Walk. And Repeat.

Although the initial challenge is over, you now have the daily walk of raising this child that you've prayed for. The challenge now becomes, Lord, how do I show them to seek you and love you.

You've got this. Just continue to put God first, and he will lead the way.

> *Glory ye in his holy name: let the heart of them rejoice that seek the LORD. Seek the LORD and his strength, seek his face continually.*
>
> 1 CHRONICLES 16:10-11 KJV

EPILOGUE

Writing this book has been a challenge... it has confirmed that I am an orator, not a writer... lol, but I hope that it helps at least one man out there press through their current (future) struggle.

www.ingramcontent.com/pod-product-compliance
Lightning Source LLC
Chambersburg PA
CBHW052121110526
44592CB00013B/1706